Essential Preparation for

UMAT
UNDERGRADUATE MEDICINE & HEALTH SCIENCES ADMISSION TEST

Series Two

2

BOOK 2
UNDERSTANDING PEOPLE

Mohan Dhall

Five Senses Education Pty Ltd
2/195 Prospect Highway
Seven Hills 2147
New South Wales
Australia

Dhall, Mohan
Series 2, Book 2 - Understanding People

ISBN 978-1-74130-893-8

CONTENTS

UMAT Trial Examination

Total Test Time: 180 minutes

- **Section 1: 48 Questions (70 minutes)**

- **Section 2: 44 Questions (55 minutes)**

- **Section 3: 42 Questions (55 minutes)**

This book covers Section 2

© Mohan Dhall
© Five Senses Education Pty Ltd

Section 2 – Understanding People (55 minutes)

Number of questions: 44

Time allowed: 55 minutes

Instructions to candidates

This section assesses the ability to understand and reason about people. Questions are based on a scenario, dialogue or other text representing specific interpersonal situations. The questions will assess your ability to identify, understand, and, where necessary, infer the thoughts, feelings, behaviour and/or intentions of the people represented in the situations.

Questions 1 – 2

The following extract comes from the diary of Bruce, a man whose first wife died of cancer, following a 2-year battle with the illness.

When Lyndal was first diagnosed she swore she would fight. Fight for me. Fight for us. Fight for our not-yet-born children. But over time that changed. As her body weakened so did her resolve. She wanted to freeze her eggs just in case... but she was too sick to follow through.

When she held my hand her grip was slipping. And so too my future....I wish she'd fought harder for all of us.

For a long time after her death I was afraid of loving again. Loss is such a painful first wife.

Question 1

Bruce wished Lyndal had fought harder because

    A) His future slipped away when she died
    B) His happiness was tied to Lyndal living
    C) He felt attached to Lyndal and her health
    D) He shared her vision of a future together with children

Question 2

What was Bruce afraid of?

    A) Loving again
    B) Losing a future partner
    C) Never loving again
    D) His partner's cancer killing him

Questions 3 - 5

Doctor: So, what's the problem?

Alex: That's what I thought you'd tell me!

Doctor: Haha…shoulder still not right? Let's see…. You do realise that if this needs reconstruction you should not play rugby again?

Alex: In that case I don't want surgery.

Doctor: I don't think you have much choice.

Alex: I didn't come hear to think of what I can't do. I came here to see what you, and I, *could* do.

Doctor: Hmmm… you *could* have surgery…or you *could* risk much more severe, permanent injury.

Question 3

Alex's attitude towards surgery can be described as

    A) Dismissive
    B) Concerned
    C) Anxious
    D) Embarrassed

Question 4

The doctor shows that he is

    A) Understanding and sympathetic
    B) Concerned and supportive
    C) Disinterested and pretentious
    D) Determined and uncaring

Question 5

What does rugby mean to Alex?

    A) It is a great game
    B) He cannot live without it
    C) He thinks he is needed by his team
    D) It is a part of his identity

Question 6 - 7

The following is an extract from an account by a lone parent, Lisa. She has two daughters aged 18-months and 3 years and a school-aged son.

We are the working poor. We look after our children and live on Centrelink payments. My ex- won't pay Child Support. What can I do? I do not know if he lives here any more or if he's moved to Queensland. One of his mates said he left long ago. But wherever he is, he is still a father and should support his own kids.

I'm on my own. I try my best but I can't get work looking after the girls. So I do the best I can. Once I did get an interview and they even tried me out for a few days. But Briahna, who was staying with mum, got sick and I couldn't go to work so they asked me not to come back.

Question 6

How does Lisa feel about her children's father?

    A) Hatred and anger
    B) Resignation and disappointment
    C) Hope and fear
    D) Resentment and jealousy

Question 7

The response of Lisa to her situation is one of

    A) Acceptance
    B) Hopelessness
    C) Indignation
    D) Contentment

Questions 8 -10

Trust is a coin of variable value. Every one of us is afraid every night. We never know what we will face – domestic violence, a car accident, an armed robbery, an overdose under the bridge where a revival may or may not be possible... Everyone calls us when they need help but no-one trusts us otherwise.

Sometimes my partner and I walk into the local pizza shop while on duty to get dinner. Fully kitted up with the gun, baton, capsicum and cuffs... Some people look down, some look away and some step back. Occasionally people stare. At these times I chat with my partner – light banter – but my eyes and awareness are everywhere else.

If only they knew – to keep them calm, stress is my girlfriend.

Question 8

Who is responsible for this recount?

A) A firemen
B) A soldier
C) An undercover agent
D) A policeman

Question 9

What is the importance of trust to the speaker?

A) The community should protect him because he is to be trusted
B) Trust is undervalued by community
C) Community should trust him more
D) Trust is a partnership between officials and people in the community

Question 10

What is meant by the statement '*Every one of us is afraid every night*'?

A) Domestic violence hurts the children they are meant to protect
B) Armed robbers could shoot at innocent people and officials
C) Uncertainty is scary when each choice can be dangerous
D) No one knows whether they will be called out to the scene of a car accident or domestic violence

Questions 11 – 12

Two girls are talking in a school playground at a high school. This is an extract from their conversation.

Sam	I love your hair!
Alicia	Really? I hate it!
Sam	I wish I had curly hair. I always wanted curly hair.
Alicia	Really? I always wanted straight hair!
Sam	Funny that – do you wish we could swap for a day?
Alicia	That would be cool – but can't you just curl your hair?
Sam	I tried once but it didn't look like yours.
Alicia	I straightened mine once but by the end of the day it was wavy and the next day curly.
Sam	Funny how we all want to be something that we are not.

Question 11

The tone between the girls can be described as

    A) Inquisitive and friendly
    B) Ominous and foreboding
    C) Chatty and light
    D) Interested and focused

Question 12

The line "*funny how we all want to be something that we are not*" implies that Sam

    A) Is observant
    B) Needs to know why
    C) Wants curly hair
    D) Is reflective

Questions 13 - 15

The following is an extract from a letter written by a woman, Tessie to her close friend. Mark is her partner.

I went to the GP and she said that the mole on my back needed attention. She asked me to come back the following Wednesday afternoon for a biopsy. Alarmingly, on Tuesday afternoon she called me to say that instead of doing the biopsy she would send me to a specialist. Wow! That knocked my breath out of me. So in two weeks I have the appointment. I asked Mark to come with me so that he can hold my hand. I don't think I ever told you that my mother and grandmother both died of cancer.

Question 13

How does Tessie feel about the changed appointment time?

    A) Concerned and needy
    B) Anxious and uncertain
    C) Helpless and stuck
    D) Bewildered and confused

Question 14

Why does Tessie want Mark with her?

    A) She gets cold hands when she is nervous
    B) She suspects that the biopsy results will bring bad news
    C) She needs to feel safe and supported
    D) She thinks the specialist will make her scared

Question 15

What is the meaning of Tessie's statement *"I don't think I ever told you that my mother and grandmother both died of cancer"*.

    A) It was an afterthought and means nothing
    B) There is a genetic predisposition to cancer
    C) Tessie is reflective and sees family traits emerging
    D) Tessie feels she may be at higher risk than others

Questions 16 - 17

The following is a recount from a university student, Abi talking to a counsellor.

I only got 45% and the average was 55%. That makes me so dumb. But worse – what will my parents say? The university has a policy that if you keep failing you have to show cause... Why am I there? To be honest I don't really know what I'm doing. My parents were so proud when I got into uni but it just isn't me. They said I could do whatever I liked... but when I enrolled in university I had never seen them happier.

I hate the way the lecturers talk. Everybody is on Facebook while the lecturers talk - but I can't keep up even though I try.

The other day I was in a tutorial and the tutor asked me a question. I hadn't done the reading so I said, "pass". Everybody laughed. And outside a bird landed on a tree and then flew away. I was that bird a long time ago.

Question 16

How does Abi perceive her parents?

    A) Very vested in her university success
    B) As a source of significant academic pressure
    C) They do not understand her
    D) They think she is not very smart

Question 17

Abi is best described as feeling

    A) Trapped
    B) Forlorn
    C) Lost
    D) Misplaced

Questions 18 - 20

Two men were talking in a pub. This conversation is an account of their conversation, but all names have been changed to protect the identity of the parties.

Geoff	Well – now I've seen it all!
Tony	Yeah...?
Geoff	Today we had staff training. Not the usual stuff though. This was a beauty! So, HR* comes down and says, "from Monday, Mark is to be called Maria". So we said, "Um...okay..." Pretty weird eh? Suddenly saying Mark is to be called Maria, right?
Tony	What do you mean?
Geoff	Well, remember the guy I told you about who has the nail polish and the mascara? Well apparently over the weekend he's becoming a chick!
Tony	A chick?? You mean...
Geoff	Yeah – he's transgender. I mean she's transgender...I mean... You get what I'm sayin'? From Monday he's doing it – making the switch. So the HR guys said to us, "you can't discriminate against her, and you must use her name, and you have to respect her".
Tony	Wow! Um... will you get in trouble if you call her 'Mark'?
Geoff	I don't know. Just when you think you know what to do - they go and change all the rules.

*HR: Human Resources

Question 18

Why does Geoff say: *So we said, "Um...okay..."*?

    A) To emphasise the confusion in the workplace
    B) To draw attention to his next statement
    C) To highlight the unusual nature of the request by HR
    D) To give Tony a sense of the meeting

Question 19

How does Geoff feel about the issue he raised?

    A) Uncertain about how to behave
    B) Angry about how it was addressed
    C) Determined to make a difference
    D) Comfortable with change

Question 20

What is Tony's role in the conversation?

    A) Encouragement
    B) Empathy
    C) Sympathy
    D) Advocate

Questions 21 - 22

This extract relates to a son musing over the memory of his father and the family dynamics before and after his death.

"My father protected the vulnerable but ignored the strong. He could man up against the weak but hated to see strength in others. He was, simply, a bully. Ambitious, he rose quickly in business. He would have his favourites, make everyone fight against each other, then play peacemaker. Even in the family, he kept some people close and others far away.

As his child, if you did anything he didn't want you to do then you didn't exist. After all, you couldn't love him if you had a brain, or an idea or independence.

It took me too long to realise that his love of money and hard work made him afraid and untrusting of everyone. His ambition and success made him immune to compassion and humility.

He fractured the family so badly that I didn't speak to my younger brother or younger sister for years.

When he died I didn't go to my father's funeral. I felt a burden lift from me in the days following the news. Strangely though, his death brought everyone closer together. I shall never though, fully reconcile with my brother."

Question 21

How does the son remember his father?

    A) As a ruthless man
    B) As an ego-centric, driven man
    C) As a man among men
    D) As protective but selfish

Question 22

How did his father's death make the son feel?

    A) Angry
    B) Emancipated
    C) Grief
    D) Disappointed

Questions 23 - 24

Here a mother discusses her decision not to vaccinate her children.

So, they are passing a new policy saying that if my child is not vaccinated ('immunised') then they cannot go to a childcare centre. Really? Is that so the vaccinated kids don't get the illness they are meant to be immunised against?

If it works then it is *my* child at risk – not the vaccinated ones. I think that there is something else going on here. Maybe a government afraid of the pharmaceutical companies and the loss of political donations? Or maybe a powerful medical lobby?

In any case, I am a conscientious objector. I shall never vaccinate my children. I see no reason why I should. When my doctor pushes all these medicines on me I never trust what they or he 'recommends'.

Question 23

The mother's tone is best described as?

    A) Adversarial
    B) Confrontational
    C) Skeptical
    D) Hypocritical

Question 24

With respect to doctors the mother believes that

    A) They are focused on healing
    B) They have a hidden agenda
    C) They would not recommend something that is not good for children
    D) They are manipulated by pharmaceutical companies

Question 25 - 27

The following is a excerpt from a diary entry by a man who has committed himself to a spiritual life.

My family did not accept the change. They asked me how I could be so lost. But for me, I felt found. I cut my hair. I became vegetarian, then vegan. Life is so much better than death and caring is so much better than consumption. I think there is anger in almost everything we do when we are not careful and loving.

I have made many friends, but others have drifted on. I see they do not know or accept who I have become. The bank, where I used to work, seems like an empty vessel, promising wealth while watching a share price.

The wheel I am on now is so much more mobile. Instead of spinning in useless circles I now move forward.

Question 25

What does the author mean by the statement "*life is so much better than death*"?

    A) That his commitment to being a vegan is a principled decision
    B) That all people who value life should become vegans
    C) His belief is that he would never compromise his values
    D) He wants all people to follow his lead in regards to valuing life

Question 26

How could the author's feeling about the life he has be described?

    A) Reconciled
    B) Conflicted
    C) Sad
    D) Uncertain

Question 27

        "The wheel I am on now is so much more mobile".

What is the meaning of this statement to the author?

    A) He feels like he is spinning in circles
    B) He is tired of life on the merry-go-round
    C) He feels like his life is progressing rather than being stationary
    D) He feels like activity has meaning rather than being meaningless

Questions 28 - 30

Two doctors are talking together as they enter the room of a patient. The patient has undergone emergency surgery. He had been attacked and mauled while on a morning jog by three American pitbull terriers. This is a recollection by the patient of the encounter from when the doctors entered the room until when they left.

I heard them talking outside and having waited since early morning I was relieved when they arrived. They came in talking and their tone sounded friendly. They clearly liked working with one another. The thinner doctor looked at me and said "Good morning...know how to make a headline don't you?" I said hello and wanted to shake his hand but as I went to move the stitches in my shoulders and ribs pulled and I felt fire run up my side. I said. "A headline?" The taller, heavier doctor answered, "You haven't had the TV on?" It was off – but not for lack of trying. It's just that when you cannot move your arms because you have 95 stitches in your shoulders and over 50 stitches in each arm then you don't exactly feel like waving remotes around. That was before I counted the ones in my left thigh.

Earlier a nurse had offered to turn it on, but my head hurt and the wounds ached despite the medication so I declined.

The thin doctor said to the heavy one "I was once chased by a dog. I will never forget it. I ran and got away though..." He picked up a chart from the end of my bed and glanced at it, and then glanced at his watch. He turned to the heavy doctor. "Looks like he'll need shots". The heavy doctor nodded and said, "Yes...my dogs once ran onto the road. I didn't look for one second and next – would you believe it – I hear the screech of brakes. You gotta be careful to keep an eye on them. They are such a handful. Not really sure why I have them. My wife says I should take them for a run in the evenings – but, seriously?"

The skinny doctor laughed and said, "Yeah well you could lose a couple of kay-gees". I was wondering how long this would last. How long I would be lying there. What the shot I needed was. "Probably more than a couple" said the fatter doctor. I pictured myself giving the shots and calling them too. As they left they were still taking about weight loss and I was left wondering.

Question 28

How could the attitude of the doctors be described?

  A) Uncaring
  B) Self absorbed
  C) Attentive
  D) Dismissive

Question 29

What does the change in adjectives used for the doctors say about the patient's feelings?

  A) He is agitated and flustered
  B) He wants to be noticed and feels unrecognised
  C) He wishes the nurse was there to treat him
  D) He is getting increasingly angry

Question 30

Why does the patient wish he *"was giving the shots and calling them too"*?

  A) He wanted the doctors to empathise with his pain and to let them know how he felt
  B) He wished he could control the doctors and hurt them
  C) He thinks that the doctors are unable to do their job so he has to do it for them by directing them
  D) He wants his shot quickly so that his pain is eased and he can recover quickly

Questions 31 – 33

A young man, Samuel who had saved for and bought his first new car is recounting his experience of finding his car badly damaged in a car park after work.

I couldn't get it. The way I parked I made sure that there was a wall beside me on one side and that I was as far away from other cars as possible. How did a car hit my car at that end of the car park? There were no security cameras at that end of the car park and when I finished late the car park was empty. There wasn't even a note on the windshield.

How could someone do that? The door, the side panel, even the bonnet is damaged. How fast did the car come around the corner? I would never do that and not tell the person.

If I found out who did it...Wow! Then there will be some damage. Now what do I do?

Question 31

Samuel could be described as being in a state of

    A) Shock
    B) Agitation
    C) Disbelief
    D) Grief

Question 32

Samuel

    A) Expects that people who damage things will pay for them
    B) Wants to find the person who did it so he can damage their car
    C) Is deeply angered that there are no security cameras
    D) Will be anxious about the cost of insurance

Question 33

What does Samuel believe he would do in the situation where his car causes damage to another one?

    A) Leave the scene without being noticed
    B) Call the police to record the damage
    C) Find the owner and give them money
    D) Disclose the incident to the owner

Questions 34 - 36

The following is a recount by a mother and father. They are describing their daughter, Julia's response to winning an award at the annual school Speech Night.

Mother   We were all there – the two of us, my mother and father, and also his (her husband's) brother and sister.

Father   Anyway, we were watching the children collect their awards and as it got closer I could see my daughter looking uneasy. Our surname is 'Vauxhall'* and so our daughter was one of the last to be called…

Mother   Then, when the third person in front of her was called Julia turned to me and said, "Mum, I can't go up there. Everyone else who got awards has really worked hard. But for me, I never tried."

Father   So I said, "Darling, just go and claim the prize. Just because you didn't try doesn't mean anything. Your teachers know you came first in this subject so go up there and stand proud"

Mother   And after that our daughter burst into tears, and no amount of encouragement would make her claim the prize. So she sat down beside us and sobbed. When they called her name and she didn't go up I was mortified….

* Names have been changed to protect the identity of the actual persons

© Five Senses Education Pty Ltd

Question 34

How does Julia feel about winning the award?

    A) Proud
    B) Ashamed
    C) Undeserving
    D) Embarrassed

Question 35

What is the father's response to his daughter?

    A) He tries to encourage her
    B) He ignores her and talks over her
    C) He knows that she is misjudging the importance of the event
    D) He feels helpless

Question 36

What does the mother feel after the daughter's name is called out, but she does not go to the stage?

    A) Exposed
    B) Protective
    C) Understanding
    D) Humiliated

Questions 37 - 38

The following is an excerpt from a conversation between a professional sportsman, Keith and his biographer.

It was tough in the beginning. They never picked me even though I knew I was better. I remember in my final year of school at the Athletics Carnival. I entered every race from the 400m and up. That included the 800m, the 1500m and the 3000m. I won each of them. But I wasn't given the prize. That went to the School Captain, Mark. He too entered many races, but in all the ones we entered together I beat him. He was from a well-known sporting family, three generations in the city. When the prize was given I felt my heart race and my hands shake.

All evening I went over the points tally – there was no doubting I won.

The next morning when I got to the school Mark came up to me and said – you should have got the prize. I said I know. Interestingly though he never told those who could make a difference. Later that year I entered competitions outside of school and really got noticed. Since that point I have never looked back.

Question 37

How did Keith feel when Mark was given the athletics prize?

    A) Angry
    B) Confused
    C) Cheated
    D) Defenceless

Question 38

What feeling best describes how Keith would have felt when Mark disclosed that he knew that Keith deserved the award he had been given?

    A) Satisfied
    B) Vindicated
    C) Understood
    D) Ambivalent

Questions 39 - 40

This is an extract from a passage written for a psychological journal but never published.

For years I lived in fear. Ever moment was accounted for. He always knew where I was, how long I would be there, who I was with, even...what I would say. When I came home my senses were hyper-alert. You could smell the air and know what to expect.

I never trusted what I heard or saw because unseen and not heard was the attitude that kept me from being myself. We had a child and for a while all was okay. But then he wanted another and another. He hated the idea of me leaving home or taking on paid work. But there was a turning point.

I had taken the girls for a walk to the shop and I was pushing the stroller with their younger brother sleeping inside. For ages I had told my husband that the wheel was a bit wobbly. Anyway, on the way a wheel fell off and stranger helped me to carry my son home. When my husband found out he hit me and said that no strange man was to enter the home. Then he refused to carry our son after that because someone else had 'displaced him".

I left, against everything I believed, six months later. Those last six months I wasn't even there. My hands were still cleaning, and my body was still working but my heart was far away.

Question 39

How would the mother have felt when a stranger helped her?

    A) Supported
    B) Valued
    C) Demeaned
    D) Sorry

Question 40

What was the main feeling the mother had for the last six months of her relationship with her children's father?

    A) Shock
    B) Distance
    C) Numbness
    D) Apprehension

Questions 41 - 42

This is a partial account from Ashwin whose brother has schizophrenia and lives as a homeless man in the town of Sheffield.

I watch these ones closely. The man who picks up cigarette butts hoping for enough to smoke. The one who buys coffee at the café and then engages in dialogue with himself all morning, every morning for hours on end. The one who wears the worn jacket and walks with bare feet, even in winter. For each of them is my brother. Each of them walks the streets of Sheffield with him, though none live in Sheffield.

I know I too could be like my brother. I had a dream once when I was working at the hospital. A voice in my dream said clearly, "You should be in Ward 10B". So the next day I went to find out what Ward 10B was. It had been closed sometime prior and there was only a Ward 10A. So I asked what Ward 10B had been. No-one knew until I found an old matron who said, "Ward 10B? That was for the maddies. The ones that no-one wants and who are a bit mental."

Such a fine line I thought, between the walking and the walking wounded.

Question 41

What is the tone of the account?

    A) Reflective
    B) Curious
    C) Protective
    D) Monotonous

Question 42

Ashwin

    A) Recognises that life is lottery and you have to take your chances
    B) Is thankful for the opportunity to be 'normal'
    C) Thinks he is lucky that he is mentally okay
    D) Understands that circumstances could have been different

Questions 43 - 44

The following is a verbal account by a mother of three who is talking about her pregnancy after adoption.

"I never thought I would have my own child or children. After years of trying, the awful miscarriages, tests upon tests upon tests and then the doctors said that it just wasn't possible. Fertility treatments are not always successful and sometimes I felt like a human laboratory. After we tried IVF* and we even thought of surrogacy. It was so complicated and there were so many issues and possible complexities that we dropped that after much thought. What if the surrogate birth mother didn't hand over the baby after the birth? I couldn't bear the thought. Surrogates might work for some couples but I would never take the chance.

So we went via DoCS* and did the whole thing – from Stage 1 to Stage 9 for Intercountry Adoption. The two-day preparation seminar was so exciting so we quickly filed an application to adopt. Then it got expensive and slow and everyone questioned our motives. It took three years to get our first child and cost over forty thousand dollars. The second was quicker, but no less expensive.

'So we are a family' I thought. At age 39 I was reconciled until I fell pregnant. I needed to be sure so I checked five times with different pregnancy kits. Then there was the issue of miscarriage arising...I thought I had my family and suddenly I wondered what could have been."

* IVF: Invitro fertilisation, DoCS: Department of Community Services

Question 43

How did the mother feel upon finding out she was pregnant?

    A) Thrilled
    B) Anxious
    C) Disbelieving
    D) Shocked

Question 44

What is the mother's view of surrogacy?

    A) It is risky and fraught
    B) It is an appropriate option for most people who cannot have children
    C) It should only be used as a last resort
    D) It helps the birth mother

ANSWERS
Summary & Worked Solutions
Multiple Choice Answer Sheet

Answers

1	D	16	A	31	C
2	B	17	D	32	A
3	A	18	C	33	D
4	B	19	A	34	C
5	D	20	B	35	A
6	B	21	B	36	D
7	A	22	B	37	C
8	D	23	A	38	B
9	C	24	B	39	B
10	C	25	A	40	B
11	A	26	A	41	A
12	D	27	C	42	D
13	B	28	B	43	C
14	C	29	D	44	A
15	D	30	A		

Answers with fully worked solutions

Question 1

D

Bruce is no longer afraid to love therefore A is incorrect. His statement 'fight for us' indicates he shared a vision with Lyndal for a family together.

Question 2

B

Tricky question! Bruce says he felt afraid of loving, but qualifies this with 'loss is such a painful first wife'. Put together and understood it is clear that Bruce was afraid of loss arising from allowing himself to love.

Question 3

A

Alex repeatedly indicates that he does not want surgery and further that he is looking for all alternative options.

Question 4

B

The doctor is not uncaring or disinterested thus C and D are clearly wrong. The doctor is not as sympathetic as supportive as he says that Alex does not have a choice and that he could risk serious injury. This indicates he has Alex's best interest in mind.

Question 5

D

Alex's insistence on not wanting surgery indicates a fear of the unknown – possible loss of his capacity to play and thus a change in identity – hence D is clearly the best response.

Question 6

B

There is nothing that indicates Lisa is aggrieved. She sounds as though she has given up on the children's father and there is a sense of passive acceptance. She is also disappointed that he is not supporting their children, thus B is the best response.

Question 7

A

Whilst her situation sounds quite desperate, Lisa does not sound hopeless. She indicates that she tries hard, 'I do the best I can' and thus demonstrates acceptance.

Question 8

D

Police officers carry the type of equipment described and undertake the duties and functions indicated thus D is correct.

Question 9

C

The police officer feels misunderstood and that the capacity to enforce the law places a barrier between him and the public. Thus he is indicating that he would like the public to trust him more.

Question 10

C

On each shift a police officer cannot know what situation they will face. They do however know that it could involve violence or facing a situation that places them in danger. In this way, the shifts are uncertain and that uncertainty is scary.

Question 11

A

The girls sound quite interested in one another and want to know each other's opinion. The tone is thus inquisitive. The better adjective is friendly rather than focused. Focused is quite a formal term and is not accurate in this context.

Question 12

D

Sam is thinking about the things people say. It may be an observation but that observation is in fact framed reflective. Thus within the term 'reflective' is the implication of observation hence D is the better response.

Question 13

B

Tessie had the 'breath knocked out of her'. She is not needy but would like the support of her partner. Thus A is not quite correct.

Question 14

C

Tessie would like the support of her partner in order to feel safe. She feels nervous and thus wants him with her.

Question 15

D

Tessie is worried that she might be at higher risk on account of the experience of her mother and grandmother. Since she has no been diagnosed a family trait cannot be definitively seen thus C is not correct. This also rules out B.

Question 16

A

Abi perceives her parents as being very proud of her. She knows that they are happy because she is at university. They do however state they want her to do what she wants to do – thus B is not correct and A is best.

Question 17

D

Abi is feeling like she should be somewhere else and that she doesn't fit in. She is not 'lost' as she has this awareness. Moreover, she is not trapped because she knows she has choice – but she does feel misplaced.

Question 18

C

The pause indicates a sense of uncertainty and that the nature of the request by HR was quite unexpected.

Question 19

A

Geoff says 'just when you think you know what to do they change the rules'. This indicates that he feels uncertain about how to behave.

Question 20

B

Tony has the unusual ability to hear what Geoff is saying and to help Geoff to clarify how he is feeling. This quality is called empathy.

Question 21

B

As his father protected the vulnerable he cannot be classified as ruthless. However he is clearly egocentric and hardworking – hence B is right.

Question 22

B

The son says he felt a weight rise off him. This indicates a feeling of freedom or 'emancipation'.

Question 23

A

The mother is very strong and is quite prepared for a fight with authorities. Of A and B, A is preferred as the tone is adversarial. Confrontational implies directly attacking an opponent whereas this is less direct and more general.

Question 24

B

Whilst D may be implied the passage suggest the government, not doctors, are influenced by the pharmaceutical companies. The whole tone is one of distrust and thus B is the best response.

Question 25

A

The reference to life follows the sentence "I became vegetarian, then vegan." C and D can be discounted as they are not evidenced in the text. His statement is about himself, not others, thus B can be ruled out. A is correct.

Question 26

A

The author sounds like he is happy with his decisions and the direction of his life – thus A is correct.

Question 27

C

The statement is followed by "Instead of spinning in useless circles…" that is – not moving forward with life. Thus, A and B are not correct as these indicate how he used to feel not how he feels now. D is too general thus C is correct.

Question 28

B

The doctors are attending the patient, albeit very casually. Thus A is not correct as is D. They are clearly interested in themselves – hence B is correct.

Question 29

D

The author is getting increasing angry as evidenced by the change in the wording from "thinner", "taller" and "heavier" to "thin" and "heavy" through to "skinny" and "fatter".

Question 30

A

The statement "*was giving the shots*", means jabbing the needle or causing some pain and the statement "*and calling them too*" means controlling what is happening. Thus, he wishes he could control the situation (NOT the doctors) and have them feel how he feels. Thus A is the best response NOT B.

Question 31

C

Samuel is in disbelief as evidenced by him saying: "I couldn't get it", "How did a car…" and "How could someone do that". These questions indicate disbelief hence C is correct.

Question 32

A

Even though he says "If I found out who did it…Wow! Then there will be some damage" this does not indicate he wants to damage the person's car. When Samuel says, "I would never do that and not tell the person" he is indicating that he expects people will be honest and to own up, and take responsibility for, damage they cause. Hence A is correct.

Question 33

D

It follows from 32 that D is correct.

Question 34

C

Julia says she did not try and the others winning awards did – hence she feels undeserving and C is correct.

Question 35

A

The father is not ignoring his daughter even though he is not actually listening well. He is trying his best to be encouraging hence A is correct.

Question 36

D

The mother places a high utility on being seen to do the right thing in public. This can been seen in her statement that she felt 'mortified' – thus D is correct.

Question 37

C

Keith clearly felt unrecognised and that the award went to the wrong person. Hence he was cheated out of it.

Question 38

B

Whilst he did not get the award he would have felt vindicated. In his mind his justification was proven correct. That is, that the person who got the award acknowledged that he (Keith) was the rightful winner.

Question 39

B

Answers A and B are very close but B is preferred as it more realistically recognises the depth of feeling the mother would have had.

Question 40

B

The mother says, "for the last six months I wasn't there", as her heart (love) was absent. She therefore felt distant rather than numb.

Question 41

A

The author is clearly observant and also insightful. This comes from being reflective, thus A is correct.

Question 42

D

There is nothing in the text indicating that Ashwin believes he must take his chances thus A is not correct. He does not express gratitude nor think he is lucky. He does however think that things might have been different for him thus D is correct and B and C are not.

Question 43

C

She was clearly disbelieving as she checked with five different pregnancy kits. She was not however 'shocked'.

Question 44

A

The mother and her partner looked at the surrogacy option and then they dropped it. This indicates that they were open but thought it too risky and uncertain thus A is correct.

Notes

Notes

Notes

Notes

Notes

Notes

Notes

Notes

42

Essential Preparation for

UMAT

UNDERGRADUATE MEDICINE & HEALTH SCIENCES ADMISSION TEST

MULTIPLE CHOICE ANSWER SHEET

Use pencil when filling out this sheet

Fill in the circle correctly

| ● | Ⓑ | Ⓒ | Ⓓ |

If you make a mistake neatly cross it out and circle the correct response

| ⊗ | ● | Ⓒ | Ⓓ |

1 Ⓐ Ⓑ Ⓒ Ⓓ
2 Ⓐ Ⓑ Ⓒ Ⓓ
3 Ⓐ Ⓑ Ⓒ Ⓓ
4 Ⓐ Ⓑ Ⓒ Ⓓ
5 Ⓐ Ⓑ Ⓒ Ⓓ
6 Ⓐ Ⓑ Ⓒ Ⓓ
7 Ⓐ Ⓑ Ⓒ Ⓓ
8 Ⓐ Ⓑ Ⓒ Ⓓ
9 Ⓐ Ⓑ Ⓒ Ⓓ
10 Ⓐ Ⓑ Ⓒ Ⓓ
11 Ⓐ Ⓑ Ⓒ Ⓓ
12 Ⓐ Ⓑ Ⓒ Ⓓ
13 Ⓐ Ⓑ Ⓒ Ⓓ
14 Ⓐ Ⓑ Ⓒ Ⓓ
15 Ⓐ Ⓑ Ⓒ Ⓓ
16 Ⓐ Ⓑ Ⓒ Ⓓ
17 Ⓐ Ⓑ Ⓒ Ⓓ
18 Ⓐ Ⓑ Ⓒ Ⓓ
19 Ⓐ Ⓑ Ⓒ Ⓓ
20 Ⓐ Ⓑ Ⓒ Ⓓ
21 Ⓐ Ⓑ Ⓒ Ⓓ
22 Ⓐ Ⓑ Ⓒ Ⓓ

23 Ⓐ Ⓑ Ⓒ Ⓓ
24 Ⓐ Ⓑ Ⓒ Ⓓ
25 Ⓐ Ⓑ Ⓒ Ⓓ
26 Ⓐ Ⓑ Ⓒ Ⓓ
27 Ⓐ Ⓑ Ⓒ Ⓓ
28 Ⓐ Ⓑ Ⓒ Ⓓ
29 Ⓐ Ⓑ Ⓒ Ⓓ
30 Ⓐ Ⓑ Ⓒ Ⓓ
31 Ⓐ Ⓑ Ⓒ Ⓓ
32 Ⓐ Ⓑ Ⓒ Ⓓ
33 Ⓐ Ⓑ Ⓒ Ⓓ
34 Ⓐ Ⓑ Ⓒ Ⓓ
35 Ⓐ Ⓑ Ⓒ Ⓓ
36 Ⓐ Ⓑ Ⓒ Ⓓ
37 Ⓐ Ⓑ Ⓒ Ⓓ
38 Ⓐ Ⓑ Ⓒ Ⓓ
39 Ⓐ Ⓑ Ⓒ Ⓓ
40 Ⓐ Ⓑ Ⓒ Ⓓ
41 Ⓐ Ⓑ Ⓒ Ⓓ
42 Ⓐ Ⓑ Ⓒ Ⓓ
43 Ⓐ Ⓑ Ⓒ Ⓓ
44 Ⓐ Ⓑ Ⓒ Ⓓ

44

Essential Preparation for

UMAT

UNDERGRADUATE MEDICINE & HEALTH SCIENCES ADMISSION TEST

MULTIPLE CHOICE ANSWER SHEET

Use pencil when filling out this sheet

Fill in the circle correctly
● (B) (C) (D)

If you make a mistake neatly cross it out and circle the correct response
⊗ ● (C) (D)

1	(A) (B) (C) (D)		23	(A) (B) (C) (D)
2	(A) (B) (C) (D)		24	(A) (B) (C) (D)
3	(A) (B) (C) (D)		25	(A) (B) (C) (D)
4	(A) (B) (C) (D)		26	(A) (B) (C) (D)
5	(A) (B) (C) (D)		27	(A) (B) (C) (D)
6	(A) (B) (C) (D)		28	(A) (B) (C) (D)
7	(A) (B) (C) (D)		29	(A) (B) (C) (D)
8	(A) (B) (C) (D)		30	(A) (B) (C) (D)
9	(A) (B) (C) (D)		31	(A) (B) (C) (D)
10	(A) (B) (C) (D)		32	(A) (B) (C) (D)
11	(A) (B) (C) (D)		33	(A) (B) (C) (D)
12	(A) (B) (C) (D)		34	(A) (B) (C) (D)
13	(A) (B) (C) (D)		35	(A) (B) (C) (D)
14	(A) (B) (C) (D)		36	(A) (B) (C) (D)
15	(A) (B) (C) (D)		37	(A) (B) (C) (D)
16	(A) (B) (C) (D)		38	(A) (B) (C) (D)
17	(A) (B) (C) (D)		39	(A) (B) (C) (D)
18	(A) (B) (C) (D)		40	(A) (B) (C) (D)
19	(A) (B) (C) (D)		41	(A) (B) (C) (D)
20	(A) (B) (C) (D)		42	(A) (B) (C) (D)
21	(A) (B) (C) (D)		43	(A) (B) (C) (D)
22	(A) (B) (C) (D)		44	(A) (B) (C) (D)

46

Essential Preparation for

UMAT

UNDERGRADUATE MEDICINE & HEALTH SCIENCES ADMISSION TEST

MULTIPLE CHOICE ANSWER SHEET

1	Ⓐ	Ⓑ	Ⓒ	Ⓓ		23	Ⓐ	Ⓑ	Ⓒ	Ⓓ
2	Ⓐ	Ⓑ	Ⓒ	Ⓓ		24	Ⓐ	Ⓑ	Ⓒ	Ⓓ
3	Ⓐ	Ⓑ	Ⓒ	Ⓓ		25	Ⓐ	Ⓑ	Ⓒ	Ⓓ
4	Ⓐ	Ⓑ	Ⓒ	Ⓓ		26	Ⓐ	Ⓑ	Ⓒ	Ⓓ
5	Ⓐ	Ⓑ	Ⓒ	Ⓓ		27	Ⓐ	Ⓑ	Ⓒ	Ⓓ
6	Ⓐ	Ⓑ	Ⓒ	Ⓓ		28	Ⓐ	Ⓑ	Ⓒ	Ⓓ
7	Ⓐ	Ⓑ	Ⓒ	Ⓓ		29	Ⓐ	Ⓑ	Ⓒ	Ⓓ
8	Ⓐ	Ⓑ	Ⓒ	Ⓓ		30	Ⓐ	Ⓑ	Ⓒ	Ⓓ
9	Ⓐ	Ⓑ	Ⓒ	Ⓓ		31	Ⓐ	Ⓑ	Ⓒ	Ⓓ
10	Ⓐ	Ⓑ	Ⓒ	Ⓓ		32	Ⓐ	Ⓑ	Ⓒ	Ⓓ
11	Ⓐ	Ⓑ	Ⓒ	Ⓓ		33	Ⓐ	Ⓑ	Ⓒ	Ⓓ
12	Ⓐ	Ⓑ	Ⓒ	Ⓓ		34	Ⓐ	Ⓑ	Ⓒ	Ⓓ
13	Ⓐ	Ⓑ	Ⓒ	Ⓓ		35	Ⓐ	Ⓑ	Ⓒ	Ⓓ
14	Ⓐ	Ⓑ	Ⓒ	Ⓓ		36	Ⓐ	Ⓑ	Ⓒ	Ⓓ
15	Ⓐ	Ⓑ	Ⓒ	Ⓓ		37	Ⓐ	Ⓑ	Ⓒ	Ⓓ
16	Ⓐ	Ⓑ	Ⓒ	Ⓓ		38	Ⓐ	Ⓑ	Ⓒ	Ⓓ
17	Ⓐ	Ⓑ	Ⓒ	Ⓓ		39	Ⓐ	Ⓑ	Ⓒ	Ⓓ
18	Ⓐ	Ⓑ	Ⓒ	Ⓓ		40	Ⓐ	Ⓑ	Ⓒ	Ⓓ
19	Ⓐ	Ⓑ	Ⓒ	Ⓓ		41	Ⓐ	Ⓑ	Ⓒ	Ⓓ
20	Ⓐ	Ⓑ	Ⓒ	Ⓓ		42	Ⓐ	Ⓑ	Ⓒ	Ⓓ
21	Ⓐ	Ⓑ	Ⓒ	Ⓓ		43	Ⓐ	Ⓑ	Ⓒ	Ⓓ
22	Ⓐ	Ⓑ	Ⓒ	Ⓓ		44	Ⓐ	Ⓑ	Ⓒ	Ⓓ